# Florals & Nature

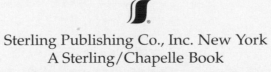
Memories of a Lifetime

Sterling Publishing Co., Inc. New York
A Sterling/Chapelle Book

Contributing designer: Paige Hill

If you have any questions or comments, please contact:
  Chapelle, Ltd., Inc., P.O. Box 9252, Ogden, UT 84409
  (801) 621-2777 • (801) 621-2788 Fax
  e-mail: chapelle@chapelleltd.com
  Web site: www.chapelleltd.com

10 9 8 7 6 5 4 3 2 1

Published by Sterling Publishing Co., Inc.
387 Park Avenue South, New York, NY 10016
© 2005 by Sterling Publishing Co., Inc.
Distributed in Canada by Sterling Publishing
c/o Canadian Manda Group, 165 Dufferin Street
Toronto, Ontario, Canada M6K 3H6
Distributed in the United Kingdom by GMC Distribution Services,
Castle Place, 166 High Street, Lewes, East Sussex, England BN7 1XU
Distributed in Australia by Capricorn Link (Australia) Pty. Ltd.
P. O. Box 704, Windsor, NSW 2756, Australia
Printed and Bound in China
All Rights Reserved

BAF ISBN 13: 978-1-4027-3925-5
    ISBN 10: 1-4027-3925-7

# Introduction

Imagine having hundreds of rare, vintage images right at your fingertips. With our *Memories of a Lifetime* series, that's exactly what you get. We've scoured antique stores, estate sales, and other outlets to find one-of-a-kind images to give your projects the flair that only old-time artwork can provide. From Victorian postcards to hand-painted beautiful borders and frames, it would take years to acquire a collection like this. However, with this easy-to-use resource, you'll have them all—right here, right now.

Each image has been reproduced to the highest quality standard for photocopying and scanning; reduce or enlarge them to suit your needs. A CD-Rom containing all of the images in digital form is included, enabling you to use them for any computer project over and again. If you prefer to use them as they're printed, simply cut them out— they're printed on one side only.

Perfect for paper crafting, scrapbooking, and fabric transfers, *Memories of a Lifetime* books will inspire you to explore new avenues of creativity. We've included a sampling of ideas to get you started, but the best part is using your imagination to create your own fabulous projects. Be sure to look for other books in this series as we continue to search the markets for wonderful vintage images.

# How to Use this Book

## General Instructions:

These images are printed on one side only, making it easy to simply cut out the desired image. However, you'll probably want to use them again, so we have included a CD-Rom which contains all of the images individually as well as in the page layout form. The CDs can be used with both PC and Mac formats. Just pop in the disk. On a PC, the file will immediately open to the Home page, which will walk you through how to view and print the images. For Macintosh® users, you will simply double-click on the icon to open. The images may also be incorporated into your computer projects using simple imaging software that you can purchase specifically for this purpose—a perfect choice for digital scrapbooking. The reference numbers printed on the back of each image in the book are the same ones used on the CD, which will allow you to easily find the image you are looking for. The numbering consists of the book abbreviation, the page number, the image number, and the file format. The first file number (located next to the page number) is for the entire page. For example, FN01-001.jpg would be the entire image for page 1 of *Florals & Nature*. The second file number is for the top-right image. The numbers continue in a counterclockwise fashion.

Once you have resized your images, added text, created a scrapbook page, etc., you are ready to print them out. Printing on cream or white cardstock, particularly a textured variety, creates a more authentic look. You won't be able to tell that it's a reproduction! If you don't have access to a computer or printer, that's ok. Most photocopy centers can resize and print your images for a nominal fee, or they have do-it-yourself machines that are easy to use.

# Ideas for using the images:

**Scrapbooking:** These images are perfect for both heritage and modern scrapbook pages. Simply use the image as a frame, accent piece, or border. For those of you with limited time, or limited design ability, the page layouts in this book have been created so that you can use them as they are. Simply print out or photocopy the desired page, attach a photograph into one of the boxes, and you have a beautiful scrapbook page in minutes. For a little dimension, add a ribbon or charm. Be sure to print your images onto acid-free cardstock so the pages will last a lifetime.

**Cards:** Some computer programs allow images to be inserted into a card template, simplifying cardmaking. If this is not an option, simply use the images as accent pieces on the front or inside of the card. Use a bone folder to score the card's fold to create a more professional look.

**Decoupage/Collage Projects:** For decoupage or collage projects, photocopy or print the image onto a thinner paper such as copier paper. Thin paper adheres to projects more effectively. Decoupage medium glues and seals the project, creating a gloss or matte finish when dry, thus protecting the image. Vintage images are beautiful when decoupaged to cigar boxes, glass plates, and even wooden plaques. The possibilities are endless.

**Fabric Arts:** Vintage images can be used in just about any fabric craft imaginable: wall hangings, quilts, bags, or baby bibs. Either transfer the image onto the fabric by using a special iron-on paper, or by printing the image directly onto the fabric, using a temporary iron-on stabilizer that stabilizes the fabric to feed through a printer. These items are available at most craft and sewing stores. If the item will be washed, it is better to print directly on the fabric. For either method, follow the instructions on the package.

**Wood Transfers:** It is now possible to "print" images on wood. Use this exciting technique to create vintage plaques, clocks, frames, and more. A simple, inexpensive transfer tool is available at most large craft or home improvement stores, or online from various manufacturers. You simply place the photocopy of the image you want, face down, onto the surface and use the tool to transfer the image onto the wood. This process requires a copy from a laser printer, which means you will probably have to get your copies made at a copy center. Refer to manufacturer's instructions for additional details. There are other transfer products available that can be used with wood. Choose the one that is easiest for you.

# Gallery of ideas

These *Florals & Nature* images can be used in a variety of projects: cards, scrapbook pages, and decoupage projects to name a few. The images can be used as they are shown in the layout, or you can copy and clip out individual images, or even portions or multitudes of images. The following pages contain a collection of ideas to inspire you to use your imagination and create one-of-a-kind treasures.

## Mother's Day Scrapbook Page

This page was created using one of the design layouts *(shown upper right)* in this book. The photographs and title were cut to fit over existing images, allowing this scrapbook page to be personalized and completed in a matter of minutes.

Mother's Day
1947

Papier-mâché boxes come in a variety of sizes, shapes, and even colors. A favorite botanical image was glued to the box lid and embellished with metal accents and mesh ribbon. The smaller artichoke image was clipped out and attached with a foam dot to lift it off the surface.

# Artichoke Box

For this project, several vintage border sections were glued around the sides of the box, evenly spaced between metal label holders adorned with a decorative heart.

Give handmade cards a professional look by effecting a crisp, clean fold. Using a bone folder to crease the cardstock will help you achieve this look.

# The Sweetest Things Card

This delightful vintage image was matted in a very untraditional manner. A torn piece of patterned paper was sewn directly onto the cardstock and a paper doily adds a delicate touch behind the image. Metal embellishments were attached with ribbons and mini brads.

the sweetest thing

# Friendship Stool

This perfect gift of friendship can easily be created using a purchased wooden stool. If the stool is unfinished, paint and seal the wood. Use a computer imaging program to add text to desired image. Print the image onto fusible fabric sheets in mirror-image mode. Follow the package instructions and iron onto the stool. Embellish with ribbons, charms, and personalized letters.

LoVE

Being deeply loved
by someone gives
you strength; loving
someone deeply
gives you courage.
-Lau Tzu

Cherish

adore

# Pansy Scrapbook Page

Layering pages with torn paper is a popular technique in scrapbooking. Here, the accent paper was sewn into place.

The vintage pansy images were used to tie all of the page elements together. Mini brads attach the pansy border to the page, adding a bit more dimension and interest. Use one of the frame boxes to add a favorite quote or to personalize the page.

# Floral Canvas Box

This unique project can be customized by adding images onto a purchased canvas box. Print the desired images onto iron-on transfer paper in mirror-image mode. Follow package directions and iron onto the sides of the box. It helps to place a small piece of wood under the fabric to keep it flat while ironing.

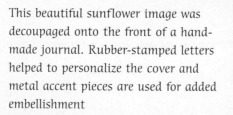

This beautiful sunflower image was decoupaged onto the front of a hand-made journal. Rubber-stamped letters helped to personalize the cover and metal accent pieces are used for added embellishment

# Garden Journal

Individual flowers were clipped out and used as photo corners for this lovely garden photograph. If your handwriting isn't all you would like it to be, use rub-on words and stickers to journal your pages.

If you choose to print out your journaling or quotes onto vellum paper, it works best if you attach it to the page with mini brads as glue tends to show through the vellum.

# Flower People Tags

These miniature works of art are fun to make and individualize. Use purchased tags or simply cut out your own. Embellish the tags with handmade papers, mesh, buttons, ribbons, and trims. Stitch around the outer edges, and attach the charming vintage "flower people" with foam dots. A sprinkling of glitter will polish off the look.

Colchicum album et rubrum. Sedum arborescens. Colchicum mixtum Autumnale

Aloe.

Ficus Indica Eystetten
sis ex uno folio enata lu,

FN01-003

FN01-002

FN01-004

FN01-005

FN01-001

FN02-003

FN02-002

FN02-004

FN02-006

FN02-005

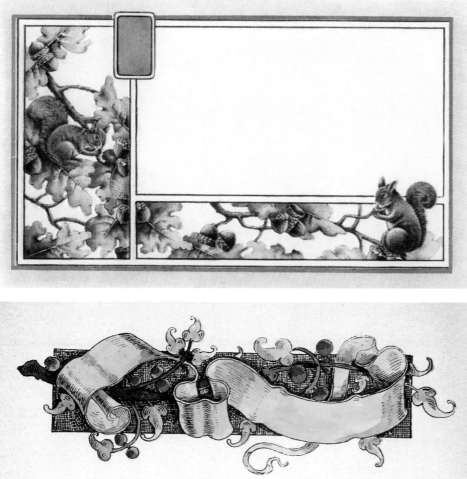

a
*friend*
might well
be reckoned the
masterpiece
of nature.

—Ralph Waldo Emerson

FN03-003                                   FN03-002


FN03-004                                   FN03-005

FN04-003

FN04-004

FN04-002

FN05-004            FN05-003            FN05-002

FN05-005            FN05-007

FN05-001            FN05-006

FN06-005                          FN06-003              FN06-002

                                      FN06-004

                    FN06-006

# Flowers are *love's* truest language.

—Park Benjamin

*I pray*, what flower's are these?
The *pansey* this, O,
that's for *Lover's* thoughts.

— George Chapman

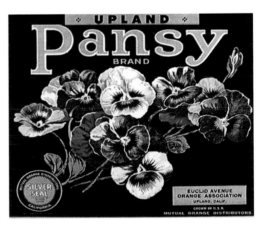

FN07-003                                    FN07-002


                    FN07-004


FN07-005


FN07-006              FN07-007              FN07-008

FN08-003                                    FN08-002




                              FN08-006










FN08-004                                    FN08-005

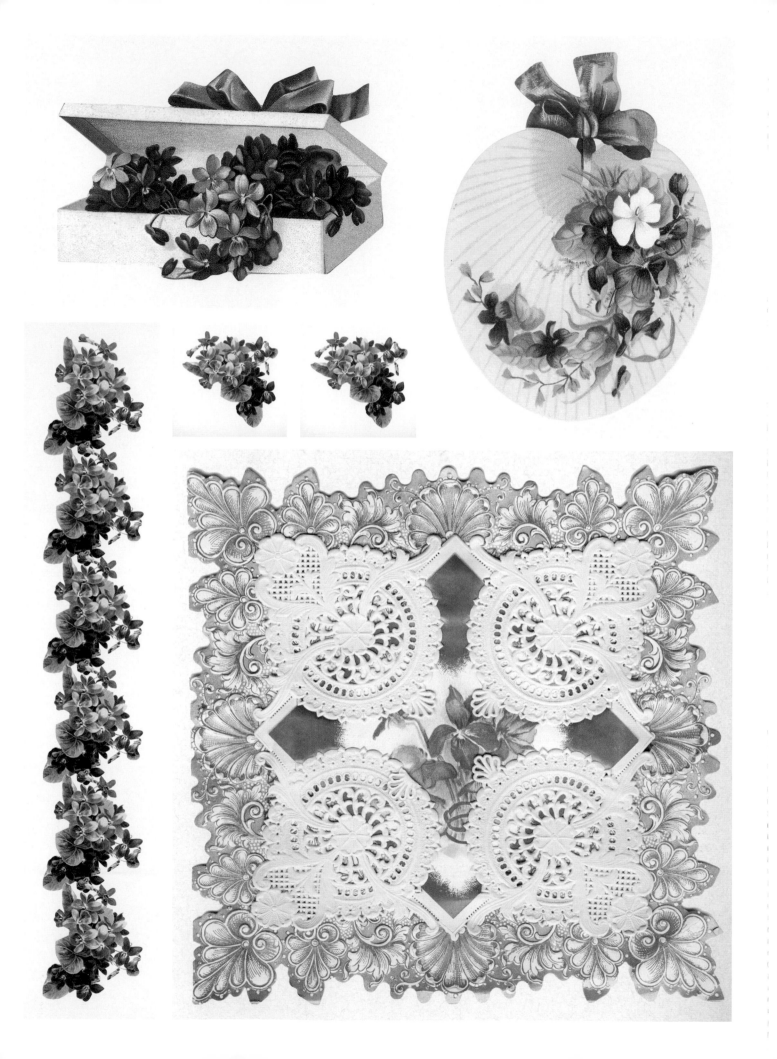

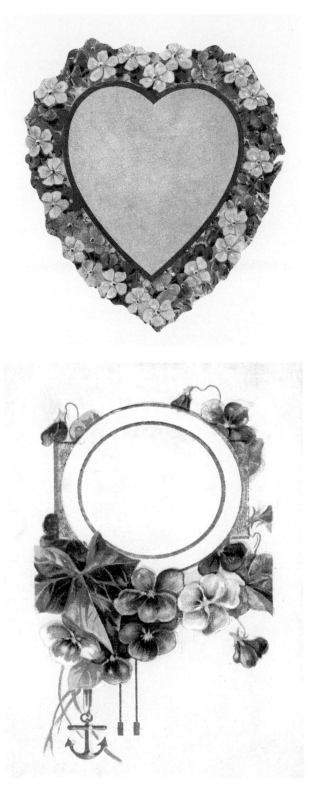

I will be the *gladdest* thing
Under the sun!
I will touch a hundred
flowers And not pick one.

— Edna St. Vincent Millay

FN09-003                                FN09-002

FN09-004

FN09-005                                FN09-007

FN09-006

FN09-001

FN10-003

FN10-002

FN10-004

FN10-005

FN10-001

Keep your Face to the Sunshine and you cannot see the Shadow.
It's what Sunflowers do.

— Helen Keller

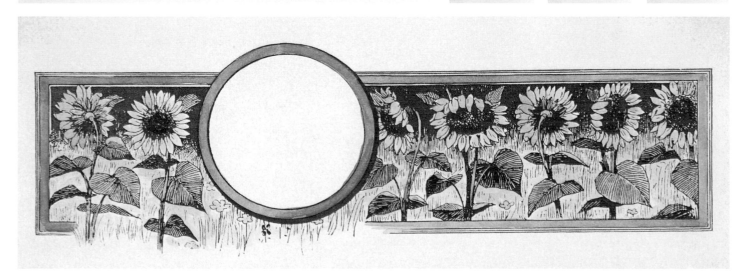

FN11-003

FN11-002

FN11-005

FN11-004

11 FN11-001

FN12-003                                    FN12-002

FN12-004                  FN12-006                  FN12-007

FN12-005

Chrysanthemum.

# THE GOLDEN AGE

CHRYSANTHÈME
DES JARDINS DOUBLE VARIÉ

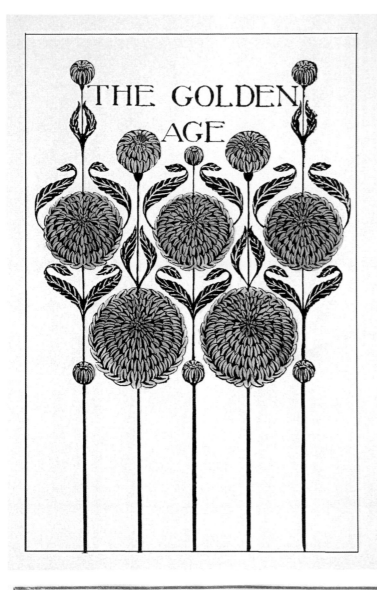

**CHRYSANTHEME**
des jardins double varié

*CHRYSANTHEMUM CORONARIUM*

Semer : 1° en mars-avril sur couche ou en pépinière
à bonne exposition ; repiquer de même et mettre en
place en mai ; 2° sur place d'avril en mai.

The *flower* that follows
the Sun does so even
on Cloudy days.

—Robert Leighton

FN13-003                                        FN13-002

FN13-004                                        FN13-006

                                                FN13-005

FN14-003                                    FN14-002




                    FN14-004

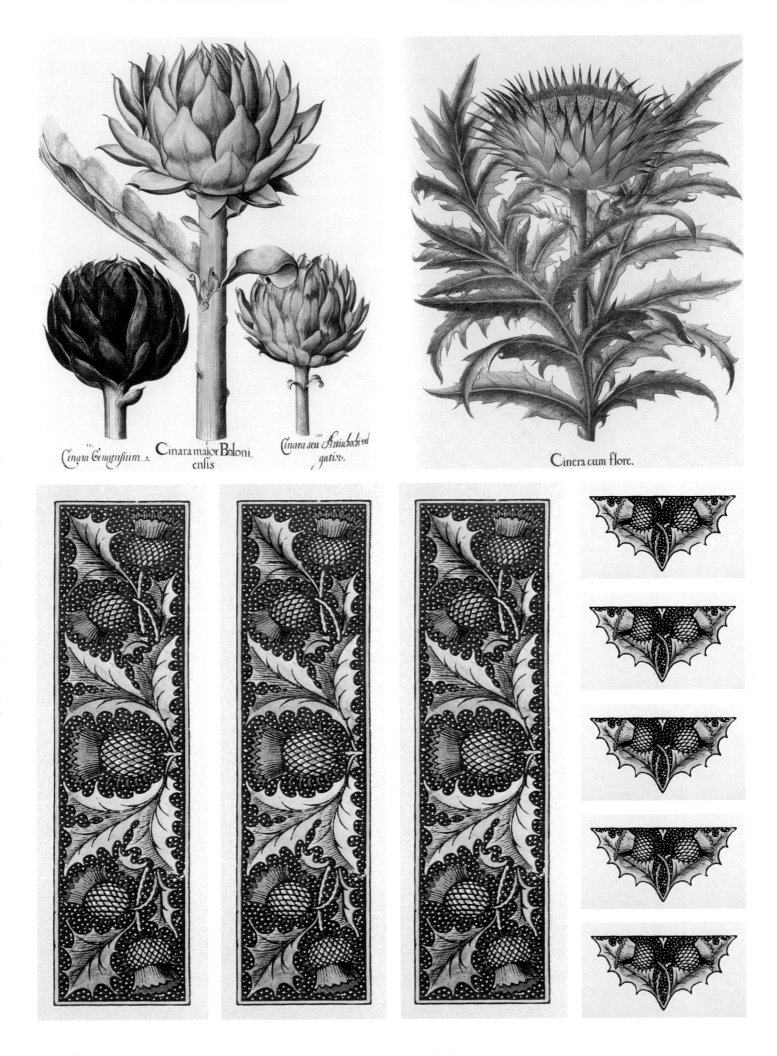

Cinara Genuensium.    Cinara maior Boloni
ensis

Cinara seu Articbochi vul
gatis.

Cinera cum flore.

FN15-003                          FN15-002

FN15-004                          FN15-005

FN16-003

FN16-002

FN16-004

Nymphæa lutea.

Nymphæa alba minor.

Nymphæa alba maior.

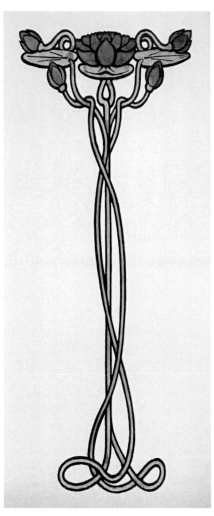

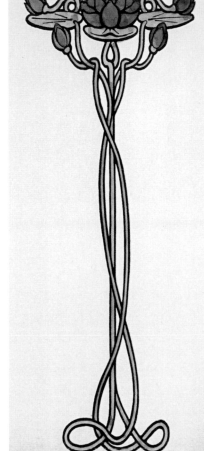

Things
*perfected*
by nature
are better
than those
finished by
ART.

— Cicero (Marcus Tullius Cicero)

FN17-003

FN17-002

FN17-004

FN17-005

FN17-006

FN18-003                                    FN18-002




FN18-004




FN18-005




FN18-006

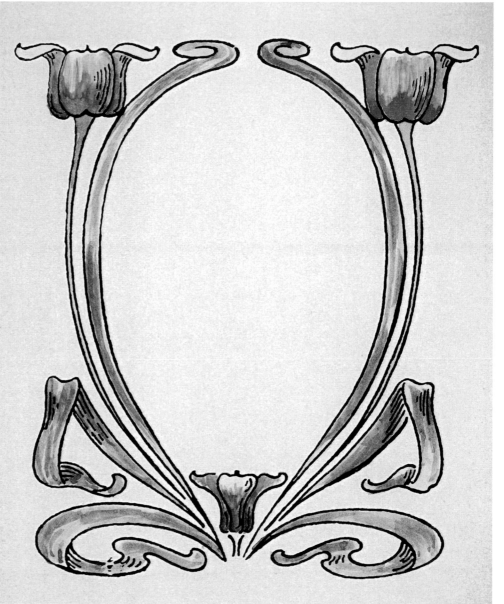

Nothing is more memorable
than a smell. One scent can be
unexpected, momentary and
fleeting, yet conjure up a
childhood summer beside a lake
in the mountains...

—Diane Ackerman

FN19-003                                    FN19-002

FN19-004                    FN19-005

FN19-001

FN20-004

FN20-003

FN20-002

FN20-005

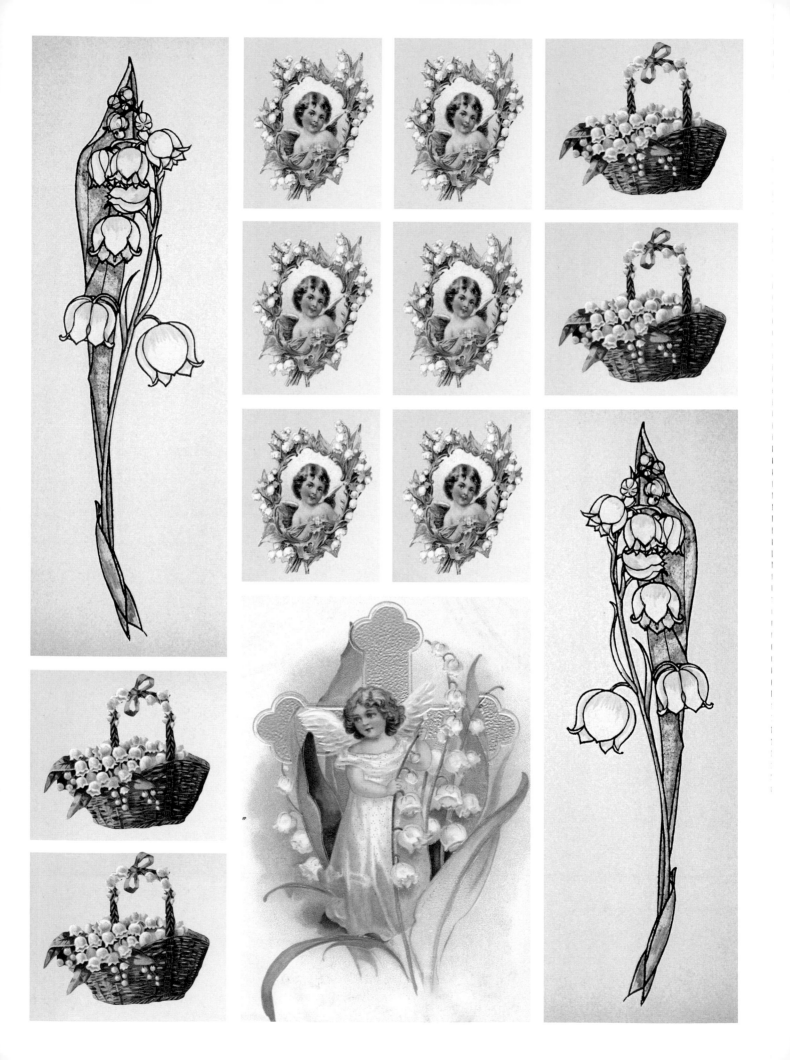

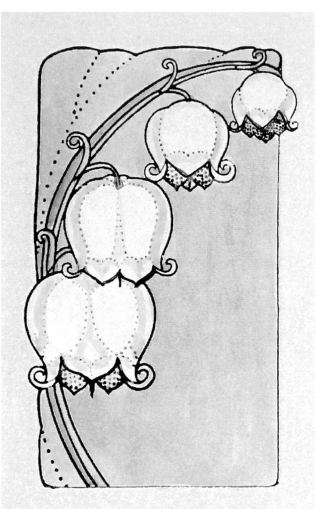

COOLING
AND
SOOTHING
**FACE
LOTION**

**BUEROMA**

THE
BUERGER
BROS.
SUPPLY
CO.

DENVER

It is at
the edge
of a petal
that *love*

waits.

— William Carlos Williams

FN21-004                    FN21-003                    FN21-002

FN21-005                                  FN21-006

FN21-001

FN22-003

FN22-004                                    FN22-002

FN22-005

FN22-006                                    FN22-007

A **morning glory**
at my window **satisfies**
me *more* than the
metaphysics of books.

— Walt Whitman

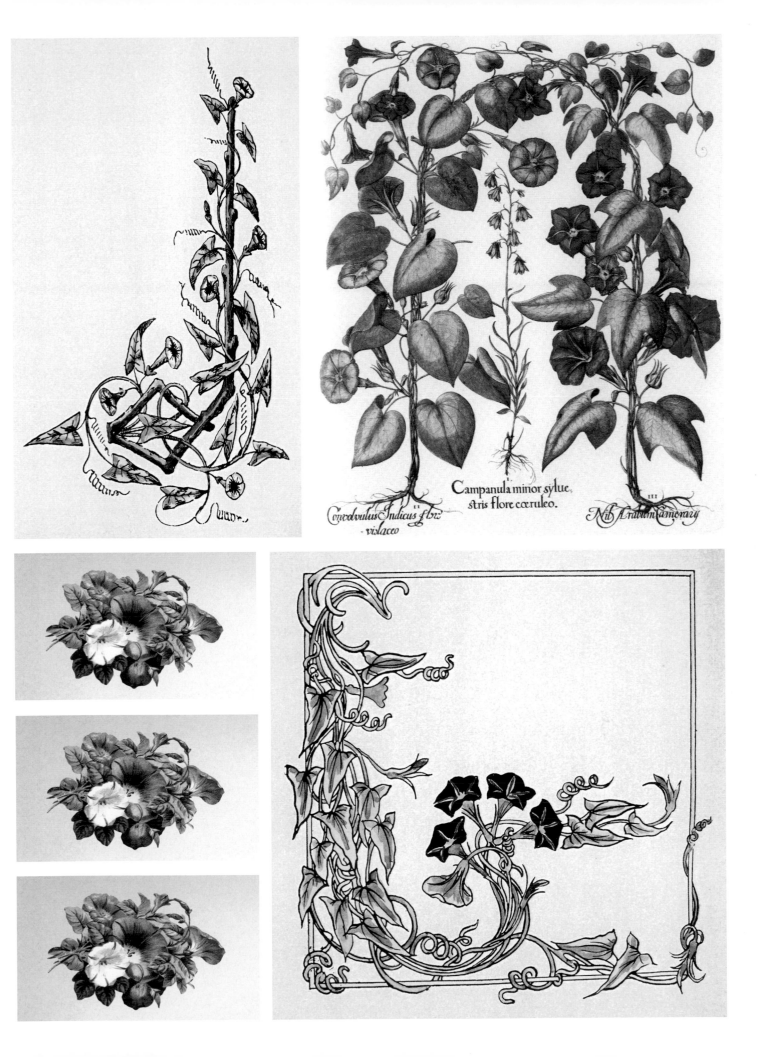

Campanula minor sylue-
stris flore cœruleo.

Conuoluulus Indicus fl.z-
violaceo

Nilsfrabicuñamoracy

FN23-003

FN23-002

FN23-004

FN23-005

FN24-003

FN24-002

FN24-004

FN24-005

FN24-006

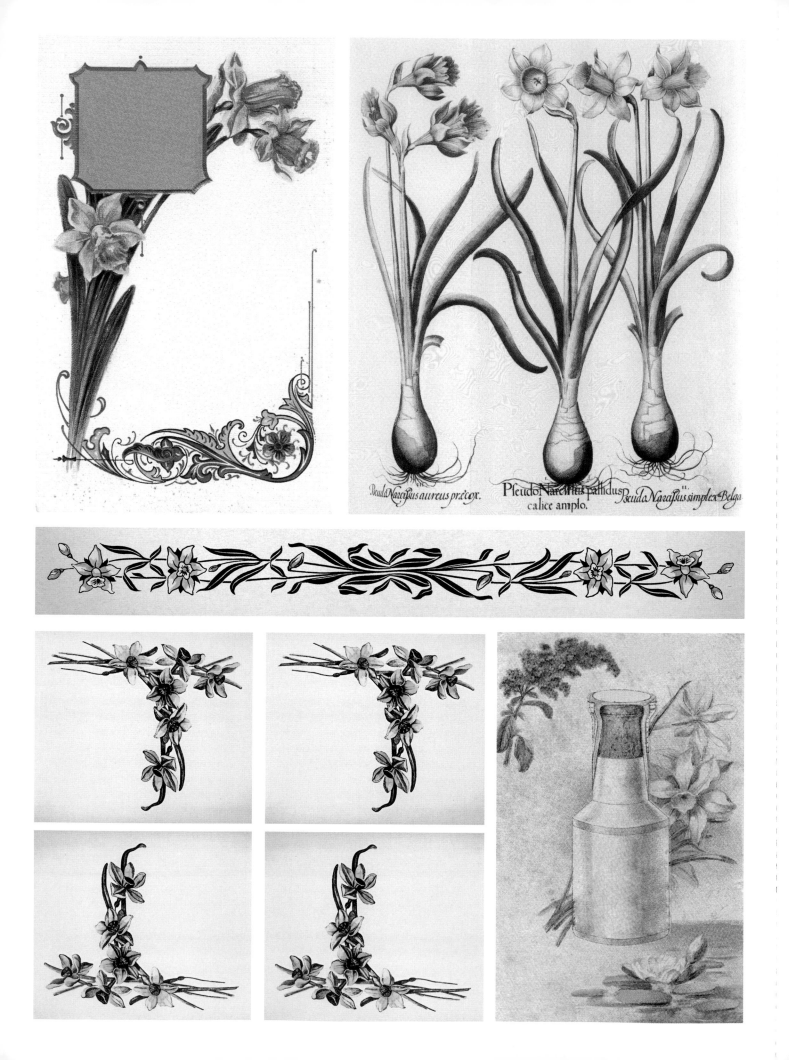

Pseuda Narcissus aureus præcox.

Pseudo Narcissus pallidus calice amplo.

Pseuda Narcissus simplex Belga

A host of

*golden daffodils:*

Beside the lake,

beneath the trees,

Fluttering and dancing

in the breeze.

— William Wordsworth

FN25-004                    FN25-003                    FN25-002

FN25-005                               FN25-006

FN26-002

FN26-003                                    FN26-005

FN26-004

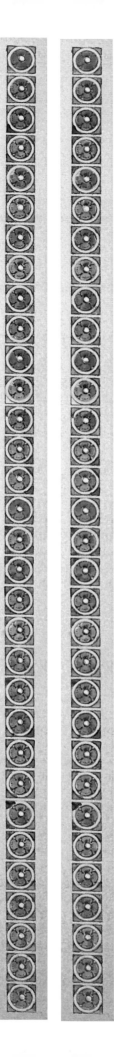

PRIMROSE
BRAND
Sugar Corn
COUNTRY GENTLEMAN

Primroses, the Spring
may love them; summer
knows but little of them.

— William Wordsword

FN27-003                                              FN27-002




FN27-004                          FN27-006




FN27-005

FN28-003                                        FN28-002




FN28-004

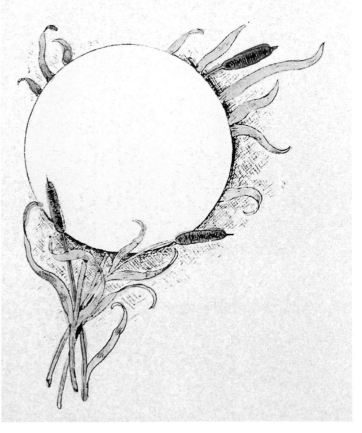

FN29-003                                    FN29-002

                                            FN29-006

FN29-004                                    FN29-005

FN29-001

FN30-001

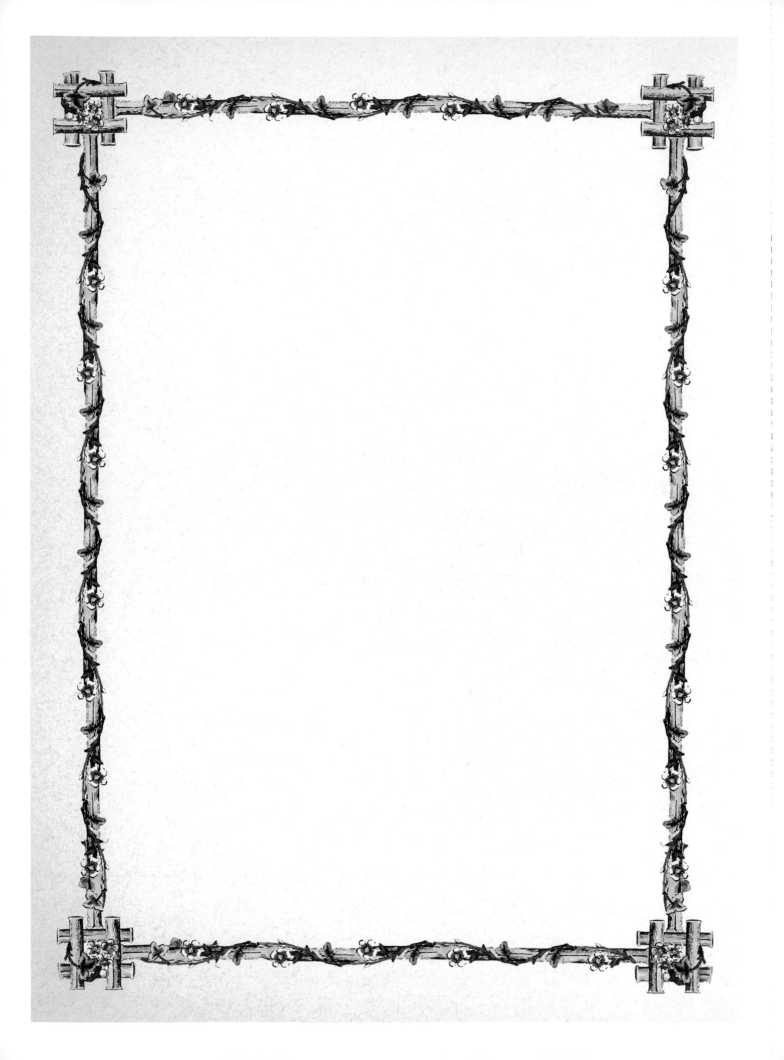

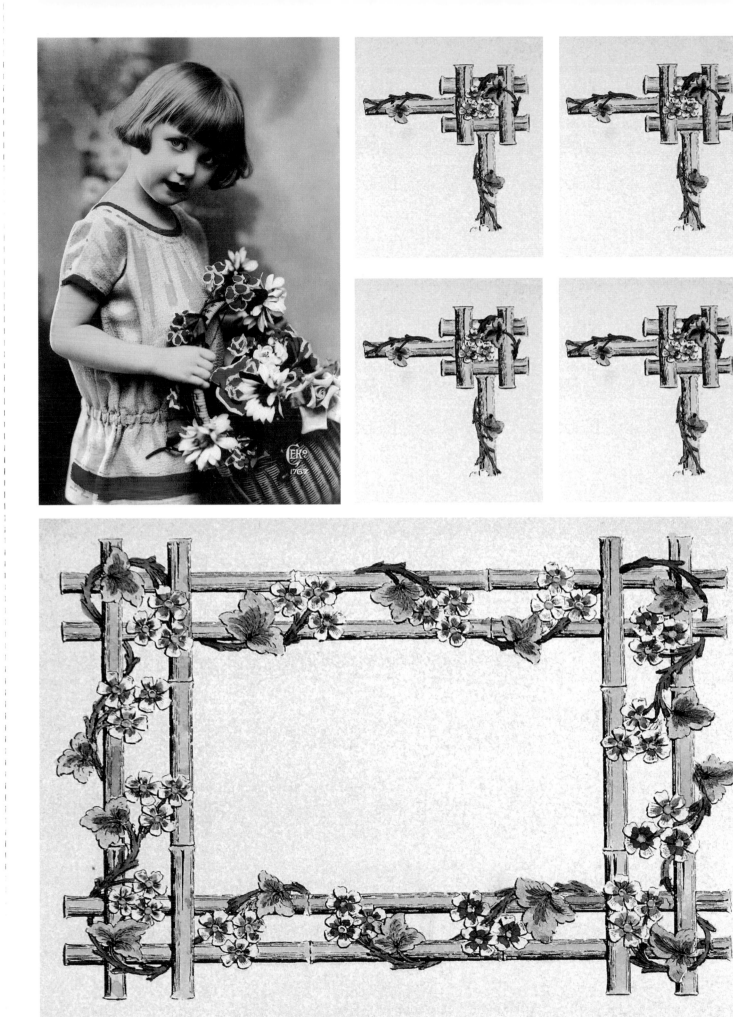

FN31-003

FN31-002

FN31-004

FN31-001

FN32-004          FN32-003                    FN32-002

                                                          FN32-005

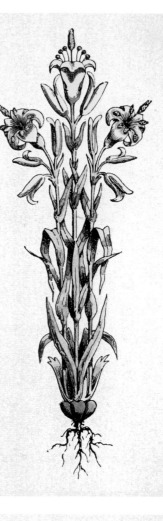

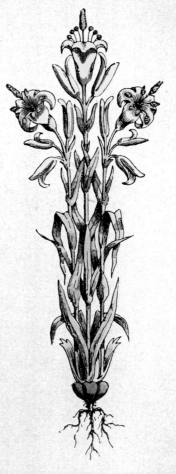

FN33-004        FN33-003        FN33-002




FN33-005        FN33-006

FN34-003

FN34-002

FN34-004

FN34-006

FN34-005

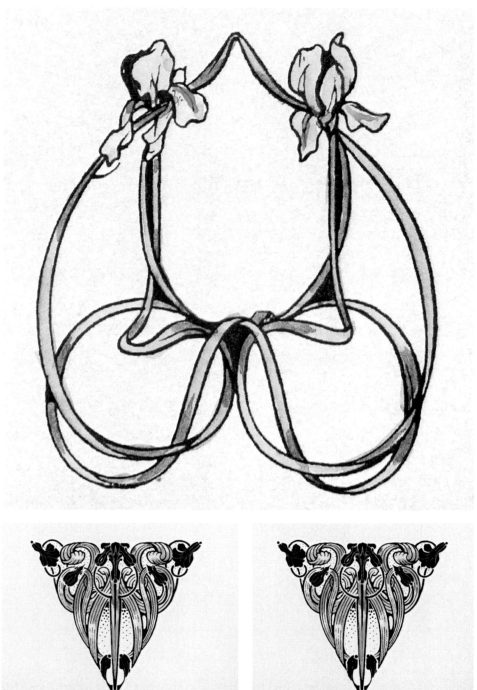

*All the*
*flowers* of
*tomorrows*
*are in the*
*seeds* of
*today.*

— Indian Proverb

Iris Florentina.

Iris Calcedonica
latifolia.

Iris Illyrica.

FN35-004          FN35-003                              FN35-002

                              FN35-007                    FN35-006

                              FN35-005

FN36-004                    FN36-003                    FN36-002

FN36-005                    FN36-006

ADDRESS

POST CARD

MESSAGE

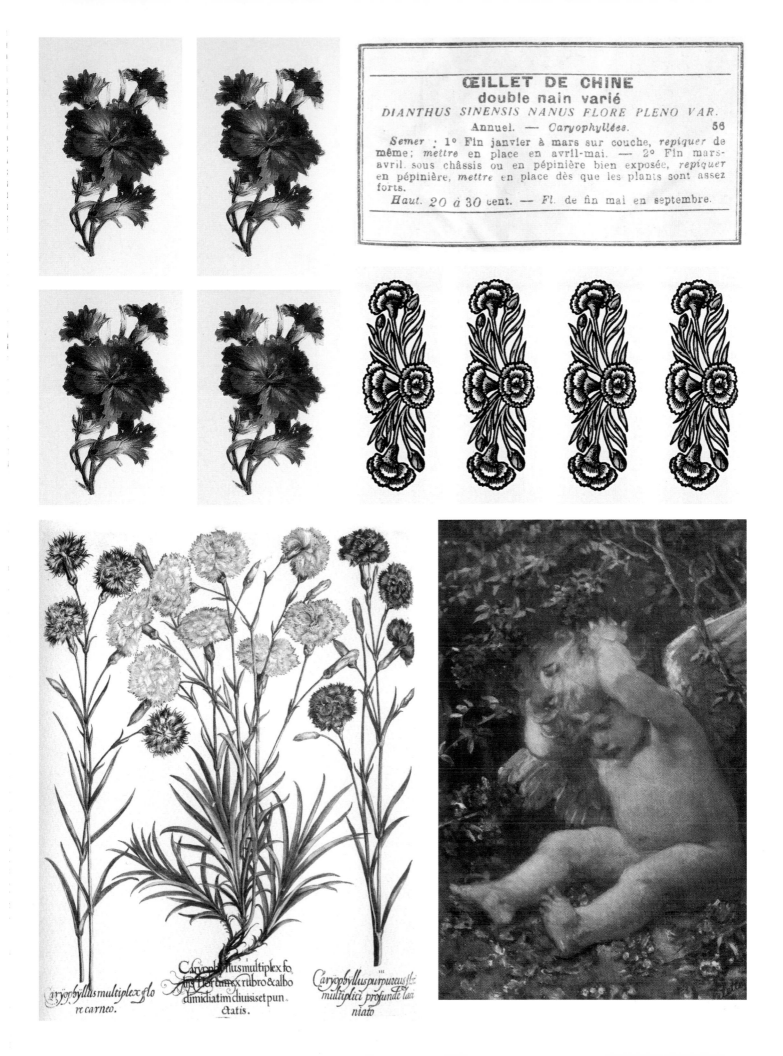

Caryophyllus multiplex flo
re carneo.

Caryophyllus multiplex fo
lijs flortim ex rubro & albo
dimidiatim diuisis et pun
ctatis.

Caryophyllus purpureus flo
multiplici profunde laci
niato

FN37-003                                          FN37-002


FN37-004


FN37-005                                          FN37-006


FN37-001

FN38-003                                    FN38-002


FN38-004


                                            FN38-007


FN38-005                                    FN38-006


FN38-001  38

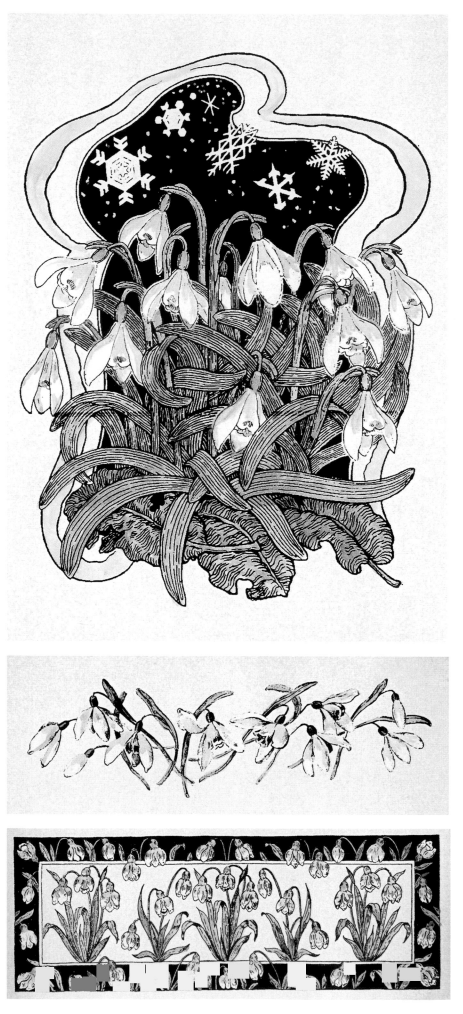

Every flower is a Soul *blossoming* in Nature.

— Gerard DeNerval

FN39-002

FN39-003                                    FN39-005

FN39-004

  FN39-001

FN40-003

FN40-004                                    FN40-002

FN40-005

FN40-007              FN40-006

FN40-009              FN40-008                    FN40-011

FN40-010

 FN40-001  40

FN41-002

FN41-004          FN41-003                    FN41-016

FN41-006          FN41-005

                                              FN41-015          FN41-014

              FN41-007                        FN41-013          FN41-012

                                              FN41-0011          FN41-0010

                                              FN41-009          FN41-008

FN42-002

FN42-003                          FN42-006

FN42-004

FN42-005

FN42-001   42

FORGET ME-NOT

MYOSOTIS BLEU DES ALPES

The blue and bright~eyed *floweret* of the brook,
Hope's gentle gem, the sweet Forget~me~not

-Samuel Taylor Coleridge

## MYOSOTIS
### des Alpes bleu
*MYOSOTIS ALPESTRIS*

Bisannuel, vivace — *Borraginées*      80

*Semer* de juillet en septembre, *repiquer* à demi-ombre
et transplanter en place en octobre-novembre à 25 cent.
de distance.

*Haut.* 20 à 30 cent.    *Fl.* abondante au printemps suivant

I am *thinking* of the lilac~trees, That shook their *purple* plumes,

And when the sash was open, Shed fragrance through the room.

— Samuel Taylor Coleridge

FN43-004                    FN43-003              FN43-002


FN43-005


FN43-006

  FN43-001

FN44-004

FN44-003

FN44-002

FN44-005

FN44-006

FN44-001  44

Winter is an etching, spring a watercolor, summer an oil painting and autumn a mosaic of them all.

—Stanley Horowitz

FN45-001

FN46-003

FN46-002

FN46-006

FN46-004

FN46-005

FN47-003                                        FN47-002


                                                        FN47-006




FN47-004                                 FN47-005

47  FN47-001

FN48-003

FN48-002

FN48-004

FN48-007

FN48-005

FN48-006

FN48-001 48

FN49-002

FN49-003                                    FN49-005

FN49-004

FN49-001

FN50-003                                    FN50-002


                                            FN50-005













FN50-004

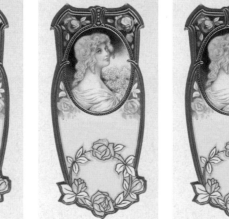

FN51-003                                        FN51-002




                                                FN51-004

FN52-001

Why not go out on a **limb**?
that's where the fruit is

—Will Rogers

FN53-003

FN53-002

FN53-004

FN53-006

FN53-005

FN53-001

FN54-003                                    FN54-002




FN54-004                                    FN54-006




FN54-005

Give me odorous at sunrise
a garden of **beautiful**
flowers Where I can
walk undistrubed

—Walt Whitman

Malua Rosea multiplex
flore albo

Malua Rosea multiplex
flore incarnato.

FN55-003                                        FN55-002

FN55-004                                        FN55-008

FN55-005                    FN55-006                        FN55-007

55 FN55-001

FN56-004                          FN56-003                    FN56-002

FN56-005

FN56-006                          FN56-007

FN56-001 — 56

Lilium cruentum bulbiferum.    Centaurium flos luteo

FN57-002

FN57-003                    FN57-005

FN57-004

  FN57-001